Look British—Think Yiddish

Look British — Think Yiddish

A Serious Sales Manual

Marshall Jarvie

Copyright © 2019 by Marshall Jarvie

All rights reserved. No part of this book may be reproduced in any form or by any electronic or mechanical means including information storage and retrieval systems without permission in writing from the author. The only exception is by a reviewer, who may quote short excerpts in a review.

Printed in the United States of America

To Susan, my wonderful wife and invaluable business partner.

About the Title
"Look British-Think Yiddish"

The title for this manual came about as I look British, but I am an American with Scottish Parents. Perhaps I look British because I dress somewhat more formally.

"Think Yiddish" is expressed through out this manual, but mainly in chapters 4 thru 7.

I became familiar with the word "Yiddish" because of my Jewish business friends in the decorative lighting business. Yiddish was the international language of the Jews from Central and Eastern Europe for many years and is a source of rich expressions and keen business acumen that have become woven in to the fabric of colloquial language and salesmanship lore in America.

Dating back to my teenage years, I have been very impressed with the exceptional talent of my friends from the Jewish culture.

Especially those men and women in the retail/wholesale business, Also those in the medical and law professions.

It is from these relationships throughout my life, I owe much gratitude and appreciation, both personally and professionally.

About the Cover

The Bow Tie has become my trade mark, at the January and June Dallas, International Lighting Markets.

Table of Contents

Preface. xi

Chapter 1 | Education and Part-time Jobs 1

Chapter 2 | Quality Traits for Success 5

Chapter 3 | Seeking Permanent Employment 9

Chapter 4 | Setting the Stage for Sales 11

Chapter 5 | The Sales Call 13

Chapter 6 | Learning from Management 17

Chapter 7 | Working with Customers 19

Chapter 8 | Becoming Self-Employed 23

Chapter 9 | Your Health 27

Chapter 10 | Retirement. 29

About the Author 31

Preface

The inspiration to write this sales manual is two-fold: One is my lifetime experience selling decorative lighting fixtures. Next was Dan Dickinson, Aledo, Texas among other business friends, who encouraged me to write a sales manual.

My approach is a proven road map for success, so I am sharing my knowledge with people contemplating a career in sales. It will work for you, providing you implement it with energy and passion.

I have often said, you can give your sales secrets to your competition, but that does not mean they would be successful. It is all about how they execute these sales techniques.

I have been fortunate to work with, and for some of the most brilliant business men in the lighting industry. Most of these men were from the Jewish Culture.

This sales manual is mainly for young people entering their sales profession, but my hope is that a seasoned sales professional will also come away with some worthwhile sales advice.

In this manual, I have made it a point to cover issues you may not learn in business school, such as, the importance of the part-time job, maintaining your health and retirement.

A successful sales career requires good planning and time management and goal setting.

Example: From the very beginning of my career as an sales representative, I have always prepared a weekly plan, listing appointments for the coming weeks. Plus, developing future plans, listing those customers and prospects.

This is most interesting when I set sales goals for myself, how often the goal number later becomes a reality.

Chapter 1

Education and Part-Time Jobs

Education

For a career in sales, a college curriculum with a Business Major and a Minor in Psychology is a great combination. This gives one a solid foundation upon which to build a career in sales.

Selecting a State College within the state where you reside is a good choice. It is cost effective and very adequate for a sales career.

Make it your goal to complete your college requirements and get your degree. If not, you may have regrets later in life.

Example: In my Junior year of college, I thought of taking a high paying job in Alaska on a fishing boat. Fortunately a professor persuaded me to stay in college and complete my requirements for graduation.

Part Time Jobs

I strongly believe in part time jobs while attending high school and college. The earlier you start the part time jobs the better. You must find time for both homework and part time job. It will be your taste of the "The Real World."

During your time with the part time jobs, you may not find jobs you will like. But, very important, you will discover what you don't like.

I had part time jobs while attending high school. But, it was not until I was going to college did I find a part time job in a lighting fixture showroom.

Here's how my first part-time job came about. I was one of six college students applying for the job. After I was hired, I asked my new boss, George Stallman, why did he hire me? He said, "You were the most persistent."

I was persistent because I followed up with phone calls.

I believe it was my sales experience, plus my eagerness for part-time work that I was hired.

The salary for this job was one dollar per hour.

After graduating from college, I met with the sales manager of Seattle Lighting and was hired, mainly because of my part time experience in lighting fixture showrooms.

Education and Part-Time Jobs

This was the beginning of a "Life Time Career" in the decorative lighting business.

I worked for one year at Seattle Lighting as a showroom sales person. Then, I was hired by Lightolier, Inc. as a company sales representative, for Washington, Oregon, Idaho, and Montana. Those were the days when some sales representatives had huge territories.

If your sales plan is to be an independent sales representative, sales experience in a showroom is a wonderful background.

14 Years Working for Lightolier, Inc.

These years with Lightolier have turned out to be the highlight of my career in decorative lighting sales.

Top management at Lightolier at that time was headquartered in New York City. Management consisted of eight remarkable businessmen: some had formal education but all were New York Street Smart. By that, I mean, great product knowledge, energy, and cleverness in a most respectful way.

All of these very exceptional businessmen were from a Jewish Culture.

From these men, I learned the importance of in-depth product knowledge and the successful techniques to employ it to the sales presentation to the customer.

The sales training I received at Lightolier was ongoing, two sales workshops per year at their New York Showroom. These were two days of intensive sales training covering new products. We would break up into small training groups to discuss sales and marketing.

Topics discussed:
- New products with exclusive designs
- Job Applications
- Markets, showrooms and electrical distributors
- Specification work with architects and electrical engineers

I often say, the training I received at Lightolier is my Masters' Degree in Sales.

M. D. Blitzer, president of Lightolier, Inc.,
addresses the firm's semi-annual sales convention.

Chapter 2

Quality Traits for Success

Here are the quality traits for success:

1. **INTEGRITY:** Integrity is honesty and sincerity.

2. **POSITIVE:** It is reassuring to customers if they find you positive, confident and decisive.

3. **PATIENCE:** Different business situations often call for a lot of patience, for example, you as a sales person might have a long wait while your buyer has to wait on his customers.

4. **OPTIMISTIC:** Set optimistic goals in respect to the future.

5. **KEEPING PROMISES:** Too often people make promises and do not keep them. Make a note on your smartphone notepad.

6. **PUNCTUAL:** Allow more time arriving at your appointment. Don't keep your customer waiting.

7. **RESPECT:** It is more important to be the most respected, rather than the most liked.

8. **COMPASSION and ALTRUISMS:** I make it a point to show my concern and understanding for those less fortunate.

9. **LOW PROFILE- HIGH VISIBILITY:** Your customers like successful salesmen but dislike those who show off their success. Visibility is always being available as needed for your customers.

10. **SENSE OF HUMOR:** The ability to see you through situations as light and humorous rather than troublesome.

Quality Traits for Success

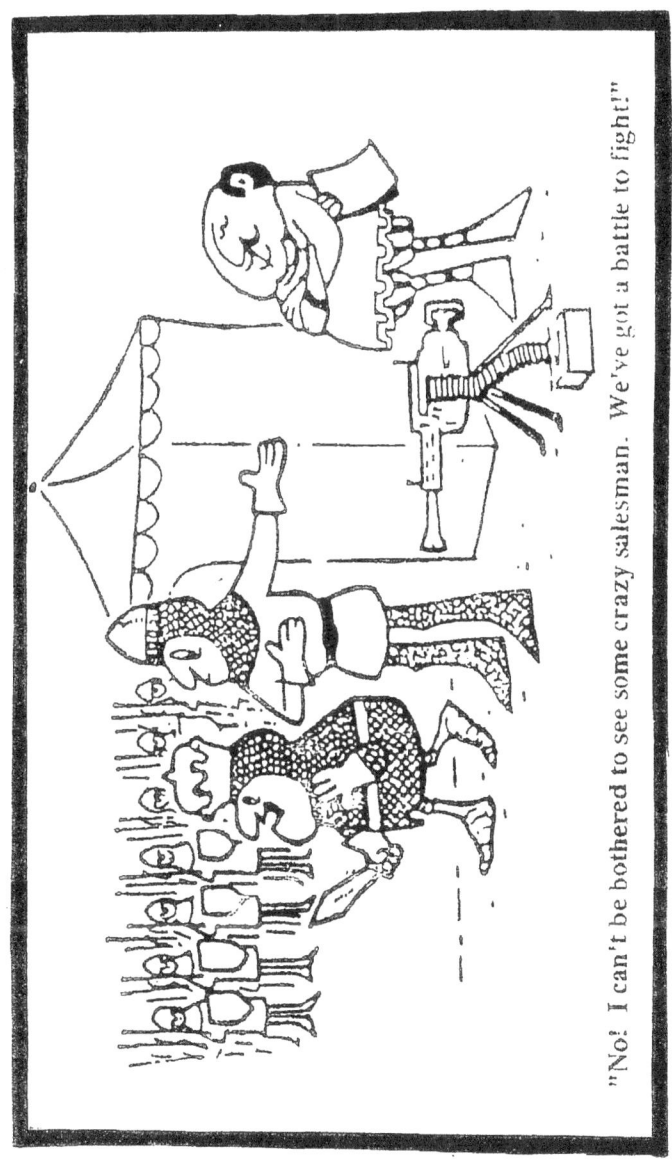

Chapter 3

Seeking Permanent Employment

By now, your education and the part time job experiences are behind you. You are now about to focus on a career in Sales.

Business Dress

While it is different today than a few years ago, it is still very important.

There is a saying, "You only have one chance for a first impression."

A good rule is dress according to your market and customers. For example: If you are working in San Francisco gray slacks, blue blazer and white dress shirt.

If in a smaller town a jacket might not be required.

Your Resume

Most often a job resume is required. I have never submitted a resume but be prepared with one.

Start at the Top

If possible, ask for a meeting either with the President or an owner of any given company. They have the time to talk and can make a decision quickly.

EXAMPLE: There was an opening at Schonbek for a California Sales Representative. I called the owner of Schonbek, Arnold Schonbek, and requested an interview with him at their headquarters in Plattsburgh, NY.

Because I had worked for Lightolier, Arnold called his dear friend, Ted Berk, at Lightolier in NY, inquiring about me. After a two-day interview with Arnold Schonbek and Bill Donaldson, I was hired as the Sales Representative for California.

Chapter 4

Setting the Stage for Sales

Your first step is making an appointment with your customer's buyer. I suggest you request an appointment one or two week in advance. Never ask for an appointment on short notice.

Very important: if your appointment is just before lunchtime, offer to take to him or her to lunch.

During lunch many good issues can be discussed, that you would not necessarily want to talk about during the sales call.

Next, have the right sales tools: A product catalog, priced out with the net cost. Your competitors also have good catalogs, so this is one of reasons why you should have samples or significant product parts on a sales call.

A "Best Sellers List" or your catalog marked with your best sellers is very important. Finally, compile your customers sales records.

Know what your customer has purchased from you in the past and be ready to tell how your products are superior to your competitors' products.

Communication with Vendors and Customers

Communication is of prime importance. In today's electronic age, you communicate with your computer, Ipad and iPhone. It is an effective and expedient way to be in touch with your vendors and customers.

Each company you represent has a website. It is usually complete with the company history, inventory, a catalog, promotions, tracking of orders and various sales rep reports.

The companies have special passwords for you and your customers to access their account on the website.

If you have done all of the above, you are ready for the next chapter, The Sales Call.

Chapter 5

The Sales Call

Before you meet with your buyer, tour their showroom. Depending on what you see, it will be helpful in your recommendations.

This is where you as a salesman play an important role with your buyer: guiding them to the best-selling items.

IMPORTANT: Begin your sales call with merchandise they have not previously purchased.

Leave what you are confident of selling for later in the call.

I have often been told that my suggestions have proven to be right. Having their confidence in your recommendations is very important.

Being a "good listener "is so important. It gives you direction in the sales presentation.

Work with your buyer as a partner "Buy with your buyer, not selling to."

Show samples, as many of you who know me, showing samples is one of the most important part of the sales call.

If the sample is an outdoor lantern or a wall a sconce, it should be lamped with a cord and plug.

Offering payment terms can be helpful in getting an order started.

Giving your customer a replacement part at no charge can get an order started.

You will not always have something new to sell. If a buyer says "What's new?" You say "Ask me what is selling"

Close the sale on a minor point. Example: May I include the right light bulbs with your fixture order?

Ask for the Order

I once traveled with a sales manager, who did a good job presenting the product, but never asked for an order!!!!

Say Thank You

Always say "Thank you "with or without an order. We send an e-mail "Thank You" for all orders.

Out of Town Travel

While traveling it is suggested that you read the local newspapers. Watch for ads for lighting by your customer and the competition, plus local projects that are being considered.

No Social Calls

Lastly, no social calls. You want your customers to know that you are meeting them to do business. However, checking in with them regularly to ask if they need some special service.

Chapter 6

Learning from Sales Management

You can receive great benefits from Sales Management and the home office.

You will find, when you make customer calls with your sales manager, your buyer will always give the two of you more visit time.

Years ago, at a Lightolier Sales Meeting in New York City, M. D. Blitzer said, "Two sales people are better than one, even if the other person is "Charlie McCarthy[*]."

Sales managers can be helpful to both you and your customer on things that you may not be permitted to do.

Example: payment terms, special pricing, a factory visit.

---

[*] Edgar Bergen, a ventriloquist, had a puppet named "Charlie McCarthy."

At this point, it is important that you and your sales manager have a meeting, before you meet with your customer on what issues are to be addressed and what are your goals.

Sometimes you may want to ask management for help with difficult topics: such as distribution and adding new accounts to a given territory.

Distribution

Proper distribution of your product, requires very careful consideration.

"Exclusives" are often one-sided, favoring your customer and not the company you represent. Personally, I prefer, "Limited Distribution" in order to receive the greatest results.

Example: Limited distribution in a small market could be one lighting showroom and one electrical wholesaler, plus one furniture store, if you have portable lamps in your sales portfolio.

Chapter 7

Working with Customers

There are several things you can do beyond just offering merchandise to sell that will make you a sales consultant

Sales Training

Sales training of your customers sales staff is one of the most important tools you can offer. For instance: both one on one training and group meetings. The best time for these meeting is usually in the morning before the store opens.

Here is something to think about:

Each of your customers has 3 or 4 people on their sales staff. You may have a total of 40 accounts. This means you have about 120 people working for you, that you do not pay.

Display Ideas

Good ideas often come from your other customers that should be passed on.

Advertising

You and the company you represent can be very helpful to your customer with advertising ideas and materials.

Often "Tie-Ins" with your company's national advertising.

Job Leads

Job leads from your company and yourself can be very important to your customer.

Job Calls

Job calls with your customer's outside sales staff is very good for them and for you.

Entertaining

I learned early on working for Lightolier, Inc. the importance of entertaining your customers.

During lunch with your buyer, you can develop a personal relationship that is not all about business. It is such a nice way to say thank you for your business. Also, other ideas are a golf game or a dinner.

Calling on Interior Designers and Architects

Making these calls on behalf of your showroom customers can generate business for them and you.

Working with Customers

If your sales portfolio is primarily decorative lighting, you will find the interior designer to be the most interested. Architects often prefer modern lighting over traditional lighting.

CAUTION: be selective and work with 20% of the industry that does 80% of the business.

These professionals are extremely busy, respect their time. "Be Brief and Be Gone."

Chapter 8

Becoming Self-Employeed

After working many years as a company salesman, and a district sales manager I decided to start my own lighting sales agency.

The big move was leaving Nutone/Lightcraft as their East Coast Sales Manager, at their offices in the Empire State Building, then relocating to Newport Beach, California.

The following will be an abbreviated summary of what transpired at Jarvie Lighting from 1967 to the present day.

I started my sales agency by representing three decorative Lighting Companies: Weiss & Biheller, Framburg, and Georgian Art Lighting.

My initial territory was the far Western States, Alaska and Hawaii.

As my business grew, I gave up territory to resident salesmen in key markets: Northern California, Washington and Oregon.

Trans Globe Lighting

1986 was the beginning of Trans Globe Lighting. While conducting my sales agency in California, a good friend and customer, Eli Haber and I decided to start our own lighting import business. Shortly after, Mark Ziv joined us making it possible to launch Trans Globe Lighting. My position at Trans Globe was a partner and National Sales Manager. After four years with TG, I decided to accept the Schonbek offer and to represent them in Florida and the Caribbean.

Not long after our move to Florida, my wife, Susan began working full time as a business partner, calling on Architects and Interior Designers.

We did this for 12 years, then returned to California. Our sales territory became International only: Central and South America, Australia, New Zealand and the Caribbean.

This is our sales territory to the present.

Your Self Employment

By now, you have acquired considerable sales experience, you are able to have lines that you hope to represent.

Major Market

I suggest that you locate in a major market. Often in a major market there would be little or no overnight travel expense. Example: Southern California

If you are not in a major market, it could require covering one or more states in order to sustain yourself financially.

Trade Markets

The Trade Markets are a good starting point in seeking out companies you would like to represent.

The Trade Markets take place usually twice a year, mid-January and mid-June.

At these markets you will meet the owners and top management. You will see their product offerings and displays.

Another option for becoming a sales representative is working for an established sales agency, as a Sub-Representative.

Look British – Think Yiddish

*Marshall Jarvie with Charlotte and Arnold Schonbek
In the Schonbek display at Farrey's
Showroom Miami, FL. 2006*

*Photo of Marshall and Susan
Schonbek Dallas showroom in the background
is Schonbek's 60" diameter Da Vinci Crystal Ball*

Chapter 9

Your Health

It's shocking, that most men take better care of their car, than they do of themselves. Example: If their car makes an unusual noise they promptly take it to their mechanic for repair.

Physical Exams

Most men do not have yearly physical checkups!

Personally, for many years I have had a yearly physical. It takes about an hour and a half. The exam includes the treadmill and body circulation.

Your Teeth

Your smile is a great asset for a sales call. Bad front teeth can spoil a smile.

According to my dentist, women pay more attention to their front teeth. If they need whitening or other dental work, they do it.

But most men will not go to the trouble or expense for their front teeth.

Years ago, I had my upper front teeth corrected with crowns. It was a big improvement, and also to my smile.

Your Hands — Men Only

About half of the people that you do business with are women.

Women take particular notice of your hands and finger nails.

It is important to keep your fingers nails well-manicured.

Chapter 10

Retirement

This is another topic that I feel strongly about.

Many years ago, a lawyer friend of mine in Newport Beach, CA said," Marshall, never retire…. You lose your deductions."

I like what my friend, the late Arthur Lebersfeld of Capitol Lighting once said, "I am semi-retired…I don't work on Sunday."

Recently I had a birthday lunch for a longtime friend, who said," I retired too early." He retired at 65 and now is 90 years old.

You must ask yourself what will I do with 20 years of retirement?

If you retire at 65, you may miss the stimulation and social contact that your career provided.

At some point, you may want to slow down or semi-retire. But Don't Stop Working!

I often say, "It's dangerous to retire."

About the Author

Born in Bellingham, Washington, October 31, 1925
Served 3 years in the Army Air Corp
Graduated from Western Washington State University
Major: Business and Minor: Psychology

Marshall at his desk
Beverly Hills, CA June 2018

My entire Sales experience has been selling decorative lighting fixtures for over 70 years. Regardless of the products you are selling, most of the "basic sales principles" apply.

This sales manual is a "road map" for both those seeking a sales career plus the experienced sales people.

It was my goal to make this manual a digest that can be read quickly, and later be reread. Too often a book is read once and put on the shelf.

My Business Philosophy

Have a healthy dissatisfaction with existing conditions.
This framed statement is on the wall above my desk.

> Have a healthy dissatisfaction for existing conditions.

END NOTES

END NOTES

www.ingramcontent.com/pod-product-compliance
Lightning Source LLC
Chambersburg PA
CBHW071151220526
45468CB00003B/1018